Penguin Education
Penguin English Project Stage One

Other Worlds
Edited by Donald Ball

Chairman: Patrick Radley

Other Worlds
Edited by Donald Ball

Things Working
Edited by Penny Blackie

Family and School
Edited by David Jackson

Ventures
Edited by Elwyn Rowlands

I Took my Mind a Walk
Edited by George Sanders

Creatures Moving
Edited by Geoffrey Summerfield

Penguin English Project

Edited by Donald Ball

Stage One Other Worlds

Penguin Books

Penguin Books Ltd, Harmondsworth,
Middlesex, England
Penguin Books Australia Ltd,
Ringwood, Victoria, Australia

First published 1971
This selection copyright © Donald Ball, 1971

Set in Monophoto Ehrhardt by
Oliver Burridge Filmsetting Ltd, Crawley, England
Printed in Great Britain by
George Pulman and Sons Ltd,
Watling Street, Bletchley, Bucks

Contents

Three Riddles

*Translated from the
Anglo-Saxon by Kevin
Crossley-Holland*
Traditional

I must fight with the waves whipped up by the wind,
Contending alone with their force combined, when I dive
To earth under the sea. My own country is unknown to me.
If I can stay still, I'm strong in the fray.
If not, their might is greater than mine:
They will break me in fragments and put me to flight,
Intending to plunder what I must protect.
I can foil them if my fins are not frail,
And the rocks hold firm against my force.
You know my nature, now guess my name.

An anchor.

Older than Adam, if Adam were still alive.
Just four weeks old, and never shall be five.

The Moon

The man that made it didn't want it.
The man that bought it didn't need it.
The man that used it didn't know it.

*~~The Moon~~
A Coffin*

Traditional English

**Questions
and Answers**

What's inside the moon?
    There's hot water inside.
What's the sky made of?
    It was made out of white snow.
If you cut the sun open what would you see?
    Terrible looking enemies.
When you write you look at your words. Have you thought
        of cutting open a letter to see what's inside?
    No. But if a person was crazy the answer would be yes.
What's inside colors?
    There's pink stars.
Where is the end of the universe?
    In back of the swimming pools.
How old is adventure?
    It is 60,000 years old.
Which color is older, black or white?
    Black because you can outline me.

Age 10
**Questions by
Vivian Tuft
Answers by
Fontessa Moore**

Problem 1   Question:
Someone
with a parcel
is running for a bus
(the parcel is very heavy).
Should he drop it?
And so make certain
of getting home all right
for sure? Or
should he struggle
with the parcel
and maybe miss the bus?
(He may
get the parcel into the bus,
which he had taken for granted
that he would,
before he suddenly saw
that he may not.)
Which then
is worse?
To arrive home
without the parcel
or to be stuck
with it
at the bus stop
and no bus?

Answer:
It depends what's in the parcel.

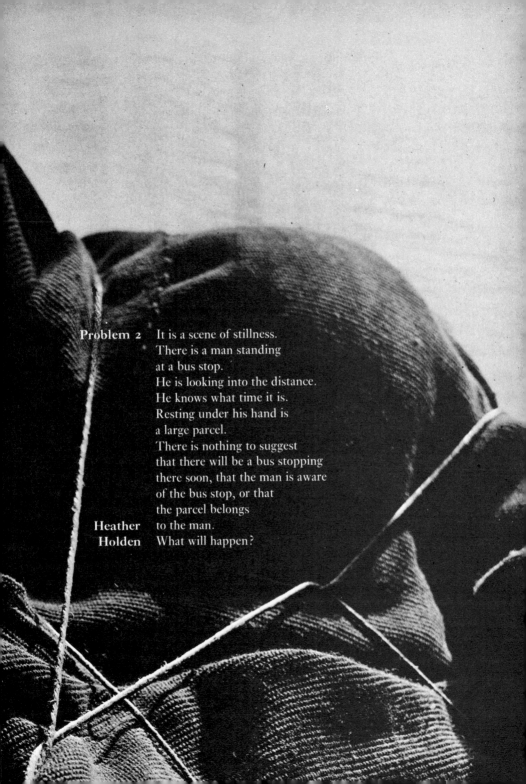

Problem 2   It is a scene of stillness.
There is a man standing
at a bus stop.
He is looking into the distance.
He knows what time it is.
Resting under his hand is
a large parcel.
There is nothing to suggest
that there will be a bus stopping
there soon, that the man is aware
of the bus stop, or that
the parcel belongs
Heather   to the man.
Holden   What will happen?

Ye Tortures

From a document found in the Archives of Bude Monastery during a squirting excavation. It shows a complete list of tortures, approved by the Ministry of Works in the year 1438, for failure to pay leg tithe, or sockage.

The prisoner will be:

Bluned on ye Grunions
   and krelled on his Grotts
Ye legges will be twergled
   and pulled thru' ye motts!

His Nukes will be Fongled
   split thrice on yon Thrulls
Then laid on ye Quottle
   and hung by ye Bhuls!

Twice thocked on the Phneffic,
   Yea broggled thrice twee.
Ye moggs will be grendled
   and stretched six foot three!

By now, if ye victim
   show not ye sorrow,
Send him home. Tell him,
   'Come back tomorrow'.

Spike Milligan

Scariboo
Translated from the
German by Max Knight
Christian
Morgenstern

The Winglewangle phlutters
through widowadowood,
the crimson Fingoor splutters
and scary screaks the Scrood.

Sounds

PLOO is breaking your shoelace.

MRRAAOWL is what cats really say.

TRIS-TRAS is scissors cutting paper.

KINCLUNK is a car going over a manhole cover.

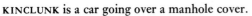

CROOMB is what pigeons murmur to themselves.

PHLOOPH is sitting suddenly on a cushion.

NYO-NYO is speaking with your mouth full.

HARROWOLLOWORRAH is yawning.

PALOOP is the tap dripping in the bath.

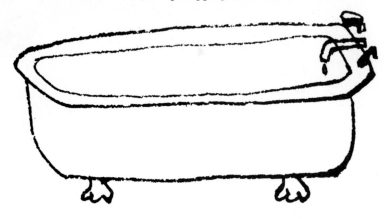

RAM TAM GEE PICKAGEE is feeling good.

Alastair Reid

Cardinal Ideograms

O **0**
O mouth. Can blow or breathe,
be funnel, or Hello.

1
A grass blade or a cut.

2
A question seated. And a proud
bird's neck.

3
Shallow mitten for two-fingered hand.

4
Three-cornered hut
on one stilt. Sometimes built
so the roof gapes.

5
A policeman. Polite.
Wearing visored cap.

6
O unrolling,
tape of ambiguous length
on which is written the mystery
of everything curly.

7
A step,
detached from its stair.

8
The universe in diagram:
A cosmic hourglass.
(Note enigmatic shape,
absence of any valve of origin,
how end overlaps beginning.)
Unknotted like a shoelace
and whipped back and forth,
can serve as a model of time.

9
Lorgnette for the right eye.
In England or if you are Alice
the stem is on the left.

10
A grass blade or a cut
companioned by a mouth.
Open? Open. Shut? Shut.

May Swenson

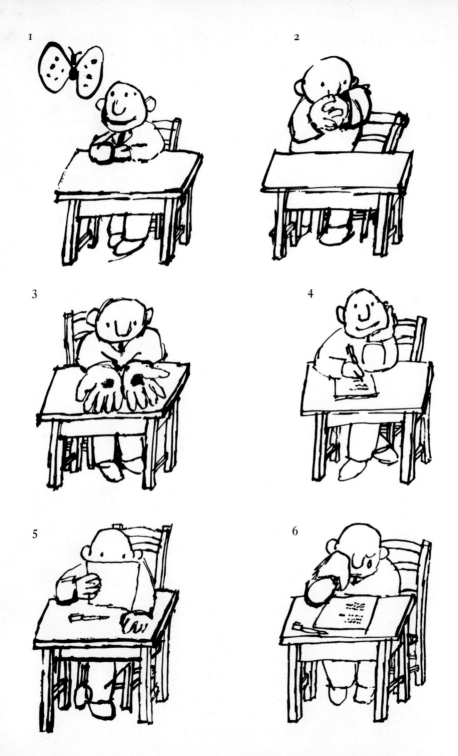

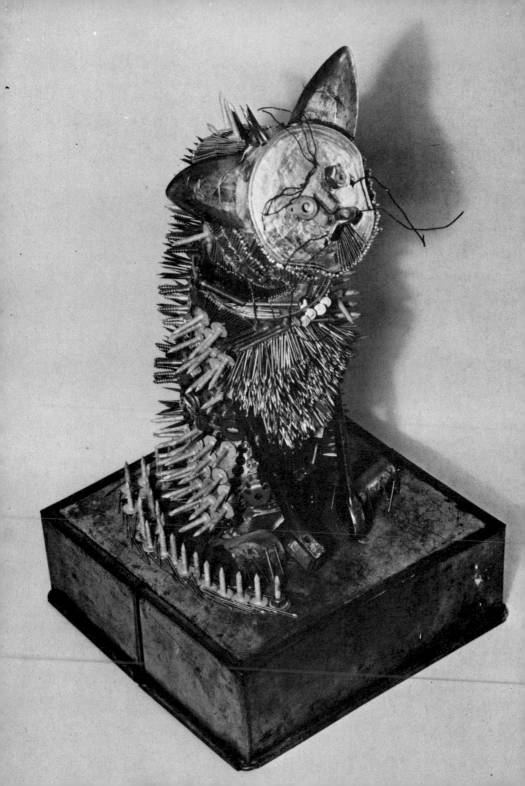

The Secret in the Cat

I took my cat apart
to see what made him purr.
Like an electric clock
or like the snore

of a warming kettle,
something fizzed and sizzled in him.
Was he a soft car,
the engine bubbling sound?

Was there a wire beneath his fur,
or humming throttle?
I undid his throat.
Within was no stir.

I opened up his chest
as though it were a door:
no whisk or rattle there.
I lifted off his skull:

no hiss or murmur.
I halved his little belly
but found no gear,
no cause for static.

So I replaced his lid,
laced his little gut.
His heart into his vest I slid
and buttoned up his throat.

His tail rose to a rod
and beckoned to the air.
Some voltage made him vibrate
warmer than before.

Whiskers and a tail:
perhaps they caught
some radar code
emitted as a pip, a dot-and-dash

of woolen sound.
My cat a kind of tuning fork? –
amplifier? – telegraph? –
doing secret signal work?

His eyes elliptic tubes:
there's a message in his stare.
I stroke him
but cannot find the dial.

May Swenson

They have yarns

They have yarns
Of a skyscraper so tall they had to put hinges
On the two stories so to let the moon go by,
Of one corn crop in Missouri when the roots
Went so deep and drew off so much water
The Mississippi riverbed that year was dry,
Of pancakes so thin they had only one side,
Of 'a fog so thick we shingled the barn and six feet out on the
fog',
Of Pecos Pete straddling a cyclone in Texas and riding it to the
west coast where 'it rained out under him',
Of the man who drove a swarm of bees across the Rocky
Mountains and the Desert 'and didn't lose a bee',

van
Of a mountain railroad curve where the engineer in his cab can
touch the caboose and spit in the conductor's eye,
Of the boy who climbed a cornstalk growing so fast he would
have starved to death if they hadn't shot biscuits up to him,
Of the old man's whiskers: 'When the wind was with him his
whiskers arrived a day before he did,'
Of the hen laying a square egg and cackling, 'Ouch!' and of
hens laying eggs with the dates printed on them,
Of the ship captain's shadow: it froze to the deck one cold
winter night,
Of mutineers on that same ship put to chipping rust with
rubber hammers,
Of the sheep counter who was fast and accurate: 'I just count
their feet and divide by four,'
Of the man so tall he must climb a ladder to shave himself,

smallest pig of a litter
Of the runt so teeny-weeny it takes two men and a boy to see
him,
Of mosquitoes: one can kill a dog, two of them a man,
Of a cyclone that sucked cookstoves out of the kitchen, up the
chimney flue, and on to the next town,
Of the same cyclone picking up wagon-tracks in Nebraska and
dropping them over in the Dakotas,
Of the hook-and-eye snake unlocking itself into forty pieces,
each piece two inches long, then in nine seconds flat snapping
itself together again,
Of the watch swallowed by the cow – when they butchered her
a year later the watch was running and had the correct time,
Of horned snakes, hoop snakes that roll themselves where they
want to go, and rattlesnakes carrying bells instead of rattles
on their tails,
Of the herd of cattle in California getting lost in a giant
redwood tree that had hollowed out,

Of the man who killed a snake by putting its tail in its mouth so
    it swallowed itself,
Of railroad trains whizzing along so fast they reach the station
    before the whistle,
Of pigs so thin the farmer had to tie knots in their tails to keep
    them from crawling through the cracks in their pens,
Of Paul Bunyan's big blue ox, Babe, measuring between
    the eyes forty-two axe-handles and a plug of Star tobacco
    exactly,
Of John Henry's hammer and the curve of its swing and his
    singing of it as 'a rainbow round my shoulder',

'Do tell!'
'I want to know!'
'You don't say so!'
'For the land's sake!'
'Gosh all fish-hooks!'
'Tell me some more.
I don't believe a word you say
but I love to listen
to your sweet harmonica
to your chin-music.
Your fish stories hang together
when they're just a pack of lies:
you ought to have a leather medal:
you ought to have a statue
carved of butter: you deserve
a large bouquet of turnips.'

Carl Sandburg

23

THE
FAR FAMED FAIRY TALE
OF
FENELLA.

A Famous Fish Factor Found himself Father of Five Fine Flirting Females, Fanny, Florence, Fernanda, Francesca, and Fenella. The First Four were Flattering, Flat Featured, Forbidden Faced, Freckled Frumps; Fretful, Flippant, Foolish, and Full of Fun. The Fisher Failed, and was Forced by Fickle Fortune to Forego his Footman, Forfeit his Forefather's Fine Fields, and Find a Forlorn Farmhouse in a Forsaken Forest. The Four Fretful Females, Fond of Figuring at Feasts in Feathers and Fashionable Finery, Fumed at their Fugitive Father, Forsaken by Fulsome, Flattering Fortune hunters, who Followed them when Fish Flourished. Fenella Fondled her Father, Flavoured their Food, Forgot her Flattering Followers, and Frolickled in Frieze without Flounces. The Father, Finding himself Forced to Forage in Foreign parts For a Fortune, Found he could afford a Fairing to his Five Fondlings. The First Four were Fain to Foster their Frivolity with Fine Frills and Fans, Fit to Finish their Father's Finances. Fenella, Fearful of Flooring him, Formed a Fancy For a Full Fresh Flower. Fate Favoured the Fish Factor For a Few days, when he Fell in with a Fog. His Faithful Filly's Footsteps Faltered, and Food Failed. He Found himself in Front of a Fortified Fortress. Finding it Forsaken, and Feeling himself Feeble and Forlorn, with Feasting, he Fed upon the Fish, Flesh, and Fowl he Found, Fricasseed and Fried, and when Full, Fell Flat on his Face on the Floor. Fresh in the Forenoon he Forthwith Flew to the Fruitful Fields, and not Forgetting Fenella, he Filched a Fair Flower, when a Foul, Frightful, Fiendish Figure Flashed Forth. " Felonious Feller, Fingering my Flower, I'll Finish you! Go! Say Farewell to your Fine Felicitious Family, and Face me in a Fortnight!" The Faint-hearted Fisher Fumed and Faltered, and Fast was Far in his Flight. His Five daughters Flew to Fall at his Feet, and Fervently Felicitate him. Frantically and Fluently he unfolded his Fate; Fenella, Forthwith Fortified by Filial Fondness, Followed her Father's Footsteps, and Flung her Faultless Form at the Foot of the Frightful Figure, who Forgave the Father, and Fell Flat on his Face; For he had Fervently Fallen in a Fiery Fit of love For the Fair Fenella. He Feasted and Fostered her, till Fascinated by his Faithfulness, she Forgot the Ferocity of his Face, Form, and Feature, and Finally, Frankly, and Fondly Fixed Friday, the Fifth day of February For the affair to come off. There were present at the wedding, Fanny, Florence, Fernanda, Francesca, and the Fisher; there was Festivity, Fragrance, Finery, Fireworks, Fricaseed Frogs, Fritters, Fish, Flesh, Fowls, and Furmity, Frontinac, Flip, and Fare, Fit For the Fastidious, Fruit, Fuss, Flambeaux, and Flowers, Four Fat Fiddlers and Fifers, and the Frightful Form of the Fortunate and Frumpish Fiend Fell From him, and he Fell at Fenella's Feet, a Fair Favoured, Fine, Frank Freeman of the Forest. Behold the Fruits of Filial affection!!

ALARMING SACRIFICE!!!

SALE BY AUCTION,

ON MONDAY NEXT, APRIL THE FIRST,

OF THE

FURNITURE & EFFECTS

OF

HOOKEY WALKER, Esq.,

Consisting of a Glass Bedstead, Iron Feather Bed and Copper Hangings, a pair of Tin Sheets, two Catgut Pillows and Lead Bolster, eight Portland Stone Night Caps, and a Green Baize Looking Glass; a brass Wire Mop with cork handle, six pounds of Moonshine, three quarts of Pigeons' Milk, four pounds of the Report of a Gun, six patent blue Buckskin Wigs lined with cold tripe; three barrels of Roasted Snow, twelve yards of Sun's Rays, a mahogany Set of China, with six Oilskin Tea Spoons, and a Muslin Milk Pot; a Sealing Wax Copper, eight Wooden Saucepans, without bottoms, sides, or tops; six pairs of Oak Gloves, a Double-Distilled Moonbeam, Flannel Tea Caddie, four pounds of Patience, six Crape Decanters with carrot corks, twelve Spider Web Wine Glasses, a Worsted Pianoforte, with Barley Sugar Keys; a Dimity Slop Pail, four Dogskin Tooth Brushes, three wings of a Lion, a case of Spiders' Eyebrows, artistically arranged; Photographs of the Buoy at the Nore, Tommy Dodd, and the Cove of Cork playing a three-cornered game of chess, a pair of Brass Boots with Leaden Straps, a pasteboard chest of Drawers, and a Tombstone made of the best pigtail Tobacco, six sky-green Shirts, a Beeswax Stove Grate with satin wood Fireirons, a Plaster of Paris Carpet, Cambric Washing Tub; two butter toasting Forks, and a decayed New Moon,

A SPLENDID OIL PAINTING,

" William the Conqueror Smoking his First Pipe of Tobacco."

And three pairs of Cotton Candlesticks, two bottles and a half of Smoke, a Calico Ale Barrel, a Brass Toad-in-the-hole, a yard of Rum-steaks cut from the Bulwarks, a set of Brown Paper Knives and Forks and a Cork Gridiron, a Paper Frying Pan, Ivory Cabbage Net, a German Sausage Watch Chain with Stilton-cheese Trinkets, a Whalebone pair of Breeches lined with Slates, a splendid pair of Gauze Bellows, a quantity of Pickled Gingerbread, two Empty Bags filled with Sand marked A.B. with the letters rubbed out, a Tallow Cheese-board, a Sable Black Horse covered with White Spots, the second-hand Report of a Cannon, a quantity of Public Opinion, in lots to suit purchasers.

UNREDEEMED PLEDGES,

The Property of several Members of Parliament, a real Live Hobby Horse, a Green Jew's Eye, some Live Butterflies stuffed with Straw, the Bower of Beauty, Six Eggs that the Ship laid-too of in the Hatchway, the name weight and colours of the Man that paid the Income Tax with pleasure, three yards of Railway Jams, a Policeman's "Move on there!" (nearly new), the Autograph of the Man in the Moon, and other articles, too numerous to mention.

Sale to Commence at half-past 5 and 20 minutes past One hour and a half.

For further particulars make an early application to the Bung-hole of the Tub with the bottom out. Conditions as usual. Carriages ordered at 13 o'clock. Horses heads to be turned inside out, and Tails made to cut their Lucky—by order of the MAYOR.

The Stunning Great MEAT PIE

A proper and pious ditty, to be taken with a peck of salt.

You've heard of the wondrous crocodile,
   And the thundering great sea snake,
No doubt it's often made you smile,
   And caused your sides to ache;
Now I've got one that'll make you laugh
   For a month to come, or nigh –
So listen while I tell you about
   A stunning great meat pie.

Now hungry folk can eat a horse –
   So I hope you'll swallow this tale,
Of the thirty-thousand-portion pie
   Cooked up in Denby Dale!

You may guess it was a tidy size,
    It took a week to make it;
A day to carry it to the shop,
    And just a week to bake it.
Oh! had you seen it, I'll be bound,
    Your wonder you'd scarce govern;
They were forced to break the front wall down
    to get it to the oven.

It took full thirty sacks of flour,
    It's a fact now that I utter,
Three hundred pails of water too,
    And a hundred tubs of butter.
The crust was nearly seven feet thick,
    You couldn't easy bruise it;
And the rolling pin was such a size
    That it took twelve men to use it!

There were twenty-five spare-ribs of pork,
    I'm sure I'm not mistaken;
With two-and-thirty hams from York,
    And twenty sides of bacon.
The pie was made by fifty cooks –
    And all of them first raters! –
And then they filled up all the nooks
    With a ton of kidney taters!

Traditional

When word was given a general rush
    Took place to hack and hew it;
They clambered up outside the crust
    To get their knives into it.
When all at once the crust gave way,
    It's true, I'll take my davy!
And ninety-five poor souls, they say,
    Were drowned in the gravy!

28

4

And in those isles are many manners of folk of divers conditions. In one of them is a manner of folk of great stature, as they were giants, horrible and foul to the sight; and they have but one eye, and that is in midst the forehead. They eat raw flesh and raw fish. In another isle are foul men of figure without heads, and they have in either shoulder one, and their mouths are round shaped like a horseshoe, y-midst their breasts. In another isle are men without heads; and their eyes and their mouths are behind in their shoulders. In another isle is a manner of folk that has a plat face, without nose or eyes; but they have two small holes instead of eyes, and they have a plat mouth, lipless. In another isle are foul men that have the overlip so great that, when they sleep in the sun, they cover all the visage with that lip. In another isle are folk of little stature, as they were dwarfs; and they are somewhat more than pygmies. They have no mouth, but they have instead of their mouth a little hole, and therefore, when they shall eat, them behoves suck it with a reed or a pipe. Tongues have they none; and therefore they speak not, but hiss and make signs as monkeys do, ilk one til other, and ilk one of them wots well what other means. In another isle are folk whose ears are so syde that they hang down to the knees. In another isle are folk that have feet like horse, and on them they will run so swythe that they will overtake wild beasts and slay them to their meat through swiftness of foot. In another isle are folk which go on their hand

flat and broad

it is necessary to

long

swift

shade

lost

certainly/truly

together

bulls

Sir John Mandeville

and on their feet, as they were four-footed beasts; and they are rough and will climb into trees als lightly as they were apes. Yet is there another isle where the folk have but a foot, and that foot is so broad that it will cover all the body and ombre it from the sun. And upon this foot will they run so fast that it is [a wonder] to see. Also there is another isle where the folk live all with the savour of a manner of apple; and if they tharned that savour, alsone they should die. Many other manner of folk there are in other isles thereabouts which were too long to tell all. For to go from isles by sea toward the east many days journeys men find a great kingdom, the which is called Mancy.

From this land men shall go to the land of Bachary, where are many wicked men and fell. In this land are trees that bear wool, as it were of sheep, of which they make cloth. In this land also are many ypotams, that dwell some time upon land and some time on the water; and they are half man and half horse. And they eat men whereso they may get them, no meat gladlier. And in that land are many griffins, more than in any country else. And some men say that they have the shape of an eagle before, and behind the shape of a lion and sickerly they say sooth. Nevertheless the griffin is more and stronger than eight lions of these countries, and greater and stalworther than a hundred eagles. For certainly he will bear til his nest flying a great horse and a man upon him, or two oxen yoked together, as they go sammen at the plough. For he has nails upon his feet als great and als long as they were oxen horns, but they are wonder sharp. And of those nails men make cups for to drink of, as we do of the horns of bugles; and of the backs of his feathers they make strong bows for to shoot with.

Moon People When Moon people grow old, they do not die. They just vanish into thin air, like smoke – and talking of smoke, I must tell you about their diet, which is precisely the same for everyone. When they feel hungry, they light a fire and roast some frogs on it – for there are lots of these creatures flying about in the air. Then, while the frogs are roasting, they draw up chairs round the fire, as if it were a sort of dining-room table, and gobble up the smoke.

That is all they ever eat, and to quench their thirst they just squeeze some air into a glass and drink that: the liquid produced is rather like dew.

Bald men are considered very handsome on the Moon, and long hair is thought absolutely revolting; but on young stars like the comets, which have not yet lost their hair, it is just the other way round – or so at least I was told by a Comet-dweller who was having a holiday on the Moon when I was there.

I forgot to mention that they wear their beards a little above the knee; and they have not any toenails, for the very good reason that they have not any toes. What they have got, however, is a large cabbage growing just above the buttocks like a tail. It is always in flower, and never gets broken, even if they fall flat on their backs.

When they blow their noses, what comes out is extremely sour honey, and when they have been working hard or taking strenuous exercise, they sweat milk at every pore. Occasionally they turn it into cheese, by adding a few drops of the honey. They also make olive oil out of onions, and the resulting fluid is extremely rich and has a very delicate perfume.

They have any number of vines, which produce not wine but water, for the grapes are made of ice; and there, in my view, you have the scientific explanation of hail storms, which occur whenever the wind is strong enough to blow the fruit off those vines.

They use their stomachs as handbags for carrying things around in, for they can open and shut them at will. If you look inside one, there is nothing to be seen in the way of digestive organs, but the whole interior is lined with fur so that it can also be used as a centrally-heated pram for babies in cold weather.

The upper classes wear clothes made of flexible glass, but this material is rather expensive, so most people have to be content

with copper textiles – for there is any amount of copper in the soil, which becomes as soft as wool when soaked in water.

I hardly like to tell you about their eyes, for fear you should think I am exaggerating, because it really does sound almost incredible. Still, I might as well risk it, so here goes: their eyes are detachable, so that you can take them out when you do not want to see anything and put them back when you do. Needless to say, it is not unusual to find someone who has mislaid his own eyes altogether and is always having to borrow someone else's; and those who can afford it keep quite a number of spare pairs by them, just in case. As for ears, the Tree-men have wooden ones of their own, and everyone else has to be satisfied with a couple of plane-tree leaves instead.

I must just mention one other thing I saw in the King's palace. It was a large mirror suspended over a fairly shallow tank. If you got into the tank, you could hear everything that was being said on the Earth, and if you looked in the mirror, you could see what was going on anywhere in the world, as clearly as if you were actually there yourself. I had a look at all the people I knew at home, but whether they saw me or not I really cannot say.

Translated from the tic by Paul Turner
Lucian

Well, that is what it was like on the Moon. If you do not believe me, go and see for yourself.

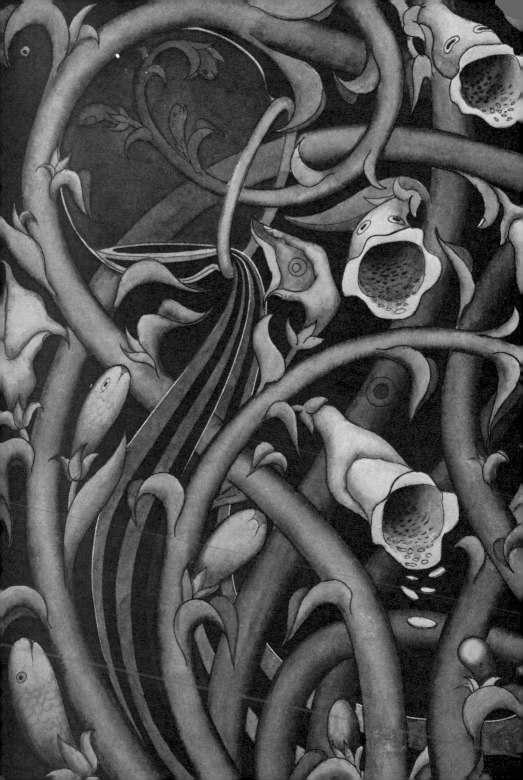

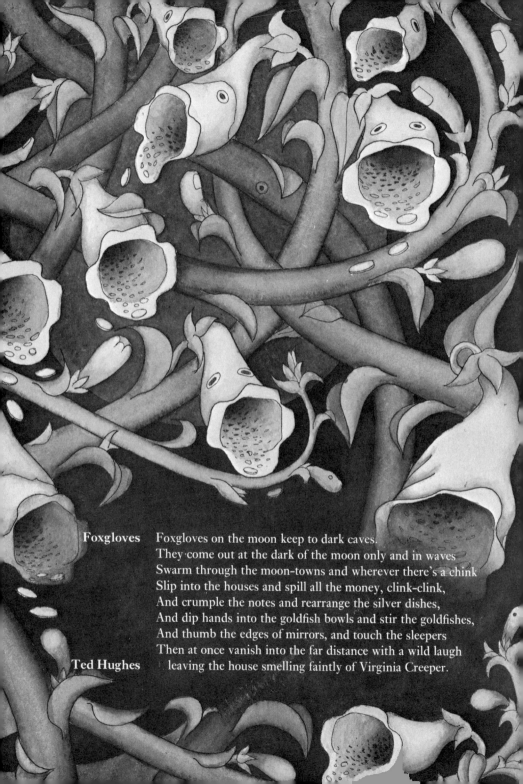

Foxgloves

Foxgloves on the moon keep to dark caves.
They come out at the dark of the moon only and in waves
Swarm through the moon-towns and wherever there's a chink
Slip into the houses and spill all the money, clink-clink,
And crumple the notes and rearrange the silver dishes,
And dip hands into the goldfish bowls and stir the goldfishes,
And thumb the edges of mirrors, and touch the sleepers
Then at once vanish into the far distance with a wild laugh
leaving the house smelling faintly of Virginia Creeper.

Ted Hughes

Locked In

All my life I lived in a coconut.
It was cramped and dark.
Especially in the morning when I had to shave.
But what pained me most was that I had no way
to get into touch with the outside world.
If no one out there happened to find the coconut,
if no one cracked it, then I was doomed
to live all my life in the nut, and maybe even die there.
I died in the coconut.
A couple of years later they found the coconut,
cracked it, and found me shrunk and crumpled inside.
'What an accident!'
'If only we had found it earlier . . .'
Then maybe we could have saved him.'
'Maybe there are more of them locked in like that . . .'
'Whom we might be able to save,'
they said , and started knocking to pieces every coconut
within reach.
No use! Meaningless! A waste of time!
A person who chooses to live in a coconut!

Translated from the　Such a nut is one in a million!
Swedish by May　But I have a brother-in-law who
Swenson　lives in an
Ingemar Gustafson　acorn

Fairy Tale

He built himself a house,
    his foundations,
    his stones,
    his walls,
    his roof overhead,
    his chimney and smoke,
    his view from the window.

He made himself a garden,
    his fence,
    his thyme,
    his earthworm,
    his evening dew.

He cut out his bit of sky above.

And he wrapped the garden in the sky
and the house in the garden
and packed the lot in a handkerchief

and went off
lone as an arctic fox
through the cold
Translated from the   unending
Czech by Ian Milner   rain
Miroslav Holub   into the world.

The Making of the Drum

The Skin

First the goat
must be killed
and the skin
stretched.

Bless you, four-footed animal, who eats rope,
skilled
upon rocks, horned with our sin;
stretch your skin, stretch

it tight on our hope;
we have killed
you to make a thin
voice that will reach

further than hope
further than heaven, that will
reach deep down to our gods where the thin
light cannot leak, where our stretched

hearts cannot leap. Cut the rope
of its throat, skilled
destroyer of goats; its sin,
spilled on the washed gravel, reaches

and spreads to devour us all. So the goat
must be killed
and its skin
stretched.

The Barrel of the Drum

For this we choose wood
of the *tweneduru* tree:
hard *duru* wood
with the hollow blood
that makes a womb.

Here in this silence
we hear the wounds
of the forest;
we hear the sounds
of the rivers;

vowels of reed-
lips, pebbles
of consonants,
underground dark
of the continent.

You dumb *adom* wood
will be bent,
will be solemnly bent, belly
rounded with fire, wound-
ed with tools

that will shape you.
You will bleed,
cedar dark,
when we cut you;
speak, when we touch you.

The Two Curved Sticks of the Drummer

There is a quick
stick grows in the for-
est, blossoms twice year-
ly without leaves;
bare white branches
crack like light-
seasonal wind   ning in the harm-
attan.

But no harm
comes to those who live nearby. This tree, the
elders say, will never
die.

From this stripped tree
snap quick sticks for
the festival. Its wood,
heat-hard as stone,
is toneless as a bone.

Gourds and Rattles

Cal-
abash trees'
leaves

do not clash;
bear a green
gourd, burn
copper in the
light, crack
open seeds
that rattle.

Blind underground the rat's
dark saw-teeth bleed
the wet root, snap
its slow long drag of time,
its grit, its flavour; turn
the ripe leaves sour. Clash
rattle, sing gourd; never leave
time's dancers weary like this tree
that makes and mocks our music.

The Gong-Gong

God is dumb
until the drum
speaks.

The drum
is dumb
until the gong-gong leads

it. Man made,
the gong-gong's
iron eyes

of music
walk us through the humble
dead to meet

the dumb
blind drum
Sky-God-Creator   where Odomankoma speaks:

Atumpan

Kon kon kon kon
kun kun kun kun
Funtumi Akore
Tweneboa Akore
Tweneboa Kodia
Kodia Tweneduru

Odomankoma 'Kyerema se
Odomankoma 'Kyerema se
oko babi a
oko babi a
wa ma ne-ho mene so oo
wa ma ne-ho mene so oo

akoko bon anopa
akoko tua bon
nhima hima hima
nhima hima hima . . .

Funtumi Akore
Tweneboa Akore
Spirit of the Cedar
Spirit of the Cedar Tree
Tweneboa Kodia

Odomankoma 'Kyerema says
Odomankoma 'Kyerema says
The Great Drummer of Odomankoma says
The Great Drummer of Odomankoma says

that he has come from sleep
that he has come from sleep
and is arising
and is arising

like *akoko* the cock
like *akoko* the cock who clucks
who crows in the morning
who crows in the morning

we are addressing you
ye re kyere wo

we are addressing you
ye re kyere wo

listen
let us succeed

listen
Edward Brathwaite   may we succeed . . .

The Making of a Monster

Found Poem: Poem found on Time Machine Toy produced by the Mattel Corporation

1 Put creature in Expansion Chamber
      until it is soft.
To see if it is soft,
      open Chamber door,
      poke creature with tongs.

When creature is soft, use tongs
      to put soft creature
      in Compressor.

2 WHEN CREATURE IS FULLY FORMED:
      Open Chamber door.
      Use tongs to take out space creature.

DO NOT USE YOUR FINGERS —
      CREATURE IS HOT!
      Let creature cool.

Albert Drake Now you can play with it.

Mr Beale He was our next-door neighbour and I had always looked upon him from a distance as a most forbidding old gentleman. But there he was now, still wearing his city uniform of black coat over his highly polished shoes. He didn't move out of the way, but stood his ground, beaming benignly down at us.

'What are you doing, sonny?' he said.

'Playing horses. I'm Black Bess. Peggy is Dick Turpin.'

'Indeed. Then I'd better be a five-barred gate. You see if you can jump over me.'

So saying, he eased his trousers up at the knees to avoid creasing them, and knelt down on all fours on the pavement before me. This strange action frightened Peggy. She dropped my reins immediately and ran off up the road, calling for me to follow her. I pretended not to hear. Mr Beale looked such a tempting five-barred gate.

I took a run and jumped.

'Well done. You just managed to clear me.'

He rose, dusted his knees and took me by the hand. Together we walked up the road. It was one of those hot dusty London evenings when every breath of air seems soiled. He led me right up to my gate, which adjoined his own.

'I suppose your Mummy will be waiting to give you your tea?' he said, as if he had enjoyed our game down the road, and was reluctant to leave me. Somehow I sensed his loneliness.

'I daresay I could stay out and play for a bit if you'll be a five-barred gate again,' I bribed.

He glanced up at my mother's windows. 'No, I don't think I can do that again here,' he said, 'but I'll tell you what we'll do. We'll go and water my flowers. I've got two watering cans. What do you say to that?'

'Yes, do let's do that,' I cried eagerly, and let him take me by the hand again and lead me up his front steps. Then, as his front door closed behind me, I remembered that Mr Beale had no garden. I stood there in his narrow hall, wondering what I should do. But I forgot my fears immediately I heard the old man running the water in his back kitchen.

'Come and get your can,' he called, adjusting the rose as he lifted a can out of the sink.

Mine was almost too heavy for me to carry. So Mr Beale took both, one in each hand.

'But where are the flowers?' I asked. 'You haven't got a garden.'

'Oh, haven't I?' he replied. 'Just you follow me.'

We went upstairs to his drawing-room.

'There,' he said, 'and I don't suppose you'll ever see such beautiful flowers though you live to be as old as I am. Mrs Beale loved lilies.'

And with that, he began to water the fleurs-de-lis patterned on his carpet.

'You do one border. I'll do the other.'

When we had emptied our cans, Mr Beale refilled them from the bathroom. After fifteen minutes the carpet was sodden.

'Haven't you any more flowers?' I asked, enjoying myself as I had never done before.

'I'm afraid not. And anyhow your Mummy will be wondering where you are. You'd better run along and have your tea; besides, I've got to get busy now and feed my animals.'

'I didn't know you had a dog.'

'I haven't.'

'A cat, then.'

'I suppose some people would call panthers cats,' he said, 'for they're the same species.' Then he mumbled a Latin name.

'I've never seen a panther,' I pleaded. 'Do let me help you feed your panthers. How many have you?'

'Two,' he replied. 'One is called Morning and the other is called Evening. And when they lie down together, the world is lonely as night.'

He spoke in the most matter-of-fact tones, rather like a school-master.

I followed him out of the room where we had watered the flowers on the carpet; and, as he shut the door behind me, I noticed that it bore the inscription 'Garden' painted neatly in the middle of one panel.

As we went downstairs to the kitchen we passed two other doors. One bore the name 'Forest' and the other 'Sea'. Bank-managers are generally methodical.

Mr Beale collected a large knuckle of beef from the larder and we immediately returned and entered the forest.

This room was entirely bare except for a scurry of rats leaving a bone which lay by the fireplace. Mr Beale didn't seem to notice the rats, which had by now disappeared behind the wainscoting. He knelt down and placed the beef beside the bare bone. Then he stood up again and lit a nightlight which was on the mantel-shelf. He placed it in a saucer of water, just as my mother did every night when she put the nightlight by my bedside. But my friend placed his in the centre of the floor. Then he drew the heavy velvet curtains which darkened the room completely.

'We must crouch in this bamboo grass,' he whispered. 'If we stay absolutely quiet, the panthers will come down from the hills and drink from that pool.'

'What pool?'

'Ssh,' he said, pointing to the little saucer of light. 'Night is very thirsty of light. And it's because these panthers drink so much that all our days get drained away.'

'You mean that if we gave them salt to eat,' I said, 'then they'd get so thirsty they'd drink so much time up that there'd be no tomorrow?'

The idea appealed to me. I never did like school.

'Exactly,' he answered. 'You at least understand. But of course you would. But you mustn't talk now or you'll frighten them away.'

We continued to squat on the floorboards.

Suddenly Mr Beale took a jack knife from his pocket and struck ferociously at the wall by his side.

'That's the second python I've killed this week,' he confided. 'They're easy to dispatch if you stab them between their eyes. Now look, the panthers are coming down now. There, beneath those mango trees. See how cruel the hard jewels of their eyes are – like emeralds of hate. And how sensuously they move on their silent paws, as though all the world were as soft as wood-ash.'

'Are they drinking the light now?' I asked.

At that moment the nightlight flickered. Perhaps a down draught from the chimney blew it out; but the forest suddenly became a blanket of darkness to me. And I screamed. Mr Beale picked me up and carried me out to the hall.

'That was a near thing,' he said, mopping his brow. 'It was just like a nightmare, only we both happened to be awake. That's the worst of life; it becomes so terrible, it leaves no terrors for our dreams. Now you must go home, or your Mummy won't let you play with me any more.'

'She doesn't know I'm here.'

'No. And don't tell her either. Or she'll never let you come fishing with me tomorrow. It's Friday tomorrow. Friday's fishing.'

It was easy for me to lie. I learned to lie as soon as I learned to talk. For I never could distinguish between what had really happened and what I had only imagined.

'We were kept late at school,' I told my Mother, 'because we had to stay and learn the song we're to sing to the parents at prizegiving; and we may be late again tomorrow,' I added, thinking of Mr Beale's promise to take me fishing.

The room bore the inscription 'Sea', and of course I made the boat from his kitchen table. We launched it by merely turning it upside down. Then we tied a teacloth across the legs at one end to serve as a sail. I remembered these legs were splintered and rough where a cat had once sharpened its claws. Mr Beale, wearing a white seaman's sweater with a roll-collar neck, rowed with a couple of furled umbrellas as oars. I acted as coxswain and tried my best to keep the nose of the boat at right angles to the breakers, to prevent us from being overturned.

'Are you a good sailor?' Mr Beale asked, labouring against the current.

I nodded apprehensively.

'Better bale out a bit,' he said, indicating an old enamelled saucepan in the prow of the boat.

I did as I was told, terrified lest we should sink and drown. And he rowed on for another ten minutes, until the sea seemed calmer, sheltered by a headland. Here we cast our lines, after baiting our hooks with imaginary bait which Mr Beale produced from a tobacco tin in his pocket.

We stayed fishing for over half an hour. I began to feel bored. I even dozed, closing my eyes and letting my line go slack.

Mr Beale seized this opportunity. 'Pull in,' he cried, waking me, 'you've got a bite.' Frantic with excitement, I pulled in my line. Two smoked kippers were fixed on the hook. I chuckled with pride.

'Can we have these for tea?' I asked.

He nodded and we promptly beached our boat and went down again to the kitchen.

Ronald Duncan

I had great difficulty in getting through the tea my Mother had prepared for me that evening. 'Peggy gave me a huge apple, and made me eat it on the way back from school,' I explained.

The Old Blind Fiddler

Beyond the alley they came to a warren of grimy streets, where old women stood in the doorways, wearing sacks for aprons, and men in carpet slippers sat on the steps. Dogs nosed among crumpled paper in the gutter; a rusty bicycle wheel lay on the cobbles. A group of boys at the corner talked to a girl whose hair was rolled in brightly coloured plastic curlers.

'I don't like this, Nick,' said Helen. 'Should we go back up the alley?'

'No. They'll think we're scared. Look as though we know where we're going – taking a short cut: something like that.'

As the children walked past, all the eyes in the street watched them, without interest or hostility, but the children felt very uncomfortable, and walked close together. The girl on the corner laughed, but it could have been at something one of the boys had said.

They went on through the streets.

'Perhaps it's not a good idea,' said Roland. 'Shall we go home?'

'Are you lost ?' said Nicholas.

'No, but –'

'Now what's all this?' said David.

Ahead of them the streets continued, but the houses were empty, and broken.

'That's queer,' said Nicholas. 'Come on: it looks as though Roland has something after all.'

'Let's go back,' said Roland.

'What, just when it's starting to be interesting? And isn't this the way to your Thursday Street?'

'Well – sort of – yes – I think so.'

'Come on, then.'

It was not one or two houses that were empty, but row after row and street after street. Grass grew in the cobbles every-where, and in the cracks of the pavement. Doors hung awry. Nearly all the windows were boarded up, or jagged with glass. Only at a few were there any curtains, and these twitched as the children approached. But they saw nobody.

'Isn't it spooky?' said David. 'You feel as if you ought to whisper. What if there was no one anywhere – even when we got back to Piccadilly?'

Helen looked through a window in one of the houses.

'This room's full of old dustbins!' she said.

'What's that chalked on the door?'

'*Leave post at Number Four.*'

'Number Four's empty, too.'

'I shouldn't like to be here at night, would you?' said Helen.

'I keep feeling we're being watched,' said Roland.

'It's not surprising,' said David, 'with all these windows.'

'I've felt it ever since we were at the map in Piccadilly,' said Roland: 'and all the way up Oldham Road.'

'Oh, come off it, Roland,' said Nicholas. 'You're always imagining things.'

'Look there,' said David. 'They've started to bash the houses down. I wonder if we'll see a demolition gang working. They do it with a big iron ball, you know. They swing it from a crane.'

Something had certainly hit the street they were in now, for only the fronts of the houses were standing, and the sky showed on the inside of windows, and staircases led up a patchwork gable end of wallpaper.

At the bottom of the row the children stopped. The streets continued, with cobbles and pavements and lamp posts – but there were no houses, just fields of rubble.

'Where's your Thursday Street now?' said Nicholas.

'There,' said David.

He pointed to a salvaged nameplate that was balanced on a brickheap. 'Thursday Street.'

'You brought us straight here, anyway, Roland,' said Nicholas. 'The whole place has been flattened. It makes you think, doesn't it?'

'There's a demolition gang!' said Helen.

Alone and black in the middle of the wasteland stood a church. It was a plain Victorian building, with buttresses and lancet windows, a steep roof, but no spire. And beside it were a mechanical excavator and a lorry.

'I can't see anybody,' said Roland.

'They'll be inside,' said Nicholas. 'Let's go and ask if we can watch.'

The children set off along what had been Thursday Street. But as they reached the church even Nicholas found it hard to keep up his enthusiasm, for there was neither sound nor movement anywhere.

'We'd hear them if they were working, Nick. They've gone home."

David turned the iron handle on the door, and pushed. The church clanged as he rattled the heavy latch, but the door seemed to be locked.

'They wouldn't leave all this gear lying around,' said Nicholas. 'They may be having a tea-break or something.'

'The lorry's engine's still warm,' said Roland. 'And there's a jacket in the cab.'

'The tailboard's down, too. They've not finished loading all this wood yet.'

'What is it?'

'Smashing up bits of pews and floorboards.'

'Let's wait, then,' said Nicholas. 'Is there anything else?'

'No – yes there is. There's a ball behind the front wheel.'

'Fetch it out, and we'll have a game.'

Roland pulled a white plastic football from under the lorry: and then he stopped.

'What's the matter?'

'Listen,' said Roland. 'Where's the music coming from?'

'What music? You're hearing things.'

'No: listen, Nick. He's right.'

A fiddle was being played. The notes were thin, and pitched high in a tune of sadness. Away from the children an old man stood alone on the corner of a street, under a broken lamp post. He was poorly dressed, and wore a crumpled hat.

'Why's he playing here?'

'Perhaps he's blind,' said Helen. 'Hadn't we better tell him where he is? He probably thinks there are houses all round him.'

'Blind people know things like that by echoes,' said David. 'Leave him alone: he may be practising. Oh, hurry up, Roland! We're waiting!'

Roland let go of the ball, and kicked it as it fell.

He was about twenty yards from the others, and he punted the ball to reach them on the first bounce: but instead it soared straight from his foot, up and over their heads so quickly that they could hardly follow it. And the ball was still gaining speed, and rising, when it crashed through the middle lancet of the west window of the church.

David whistled. 'Bullseye, Roland! Do it again!'

'Shh!' said Helen.

'It doesn't matter. They're pulling the place down, aren't they?'

'I didn't kick it very hard,' said Roland.

'Not much!'

'Never mind,' said Helen, 'I'll go and see if I can climb in.'

'We'll all go,' said David.

'No. Stay here in case the gang comes back,' said Helen, and she disappeared round the corner of the church.

'Trust you to break a window,' said Nicholas.

'I'm sorry, Nick: I didn't mean to. I just kicked the ball, and it seemed to fly by itself.'

'It flew by itself,' said Nicholas. 'Here we go again!'

'But it did!' said Roland. 'When I kicked the ball, the – the fiddle seemed to stick on a note. Didn't you hear it? It went right through my head. And it got worse and worse, all the time the ball was in the air, until the window broke. Didn't you hear the music?'

'No. And I don't now. And I don't see your fiddler, either. He's gone.'

'There's something odd, though,' said David. 'It was only a plastic ball, but it's snapped the leading in the window.'

'Oh, it was certainly a good kick from old Roland,' said Nicholas. 'And listen: your fiddler's at it again.'

The music was faint, but although the tune was the same as before, it was now urgent, a wild dance; faster; higher; until the notes merged into one tone that slowly rose past the range of hearing. For a while the sound could still be felt. Then there was nothing.

'What's Helen doing?' said Nicholas. 'Hasn't she found it yet?'

'She may not be able to climb in,' said David. 'I'll go and see.'

'And tell her to hurry up,' said Nicholas.

'OK.'

Nicholas and Roland waited.

'I never knew there were places like this, did you, Nick?'

'I think it's what they call "slum clearance",' said Nicholas. 'A lot of houses were bombed in the war, you know, and those that weren't are being pulled down to make room for new flats. That'll be why all these were empty. They're the next for the chop.'

'Where do all the people live while the flats are being built?' said Roland.

'I don't know. But have you noticed? If we'd carried on right across here, the next lot of houses aren't empty. Perhaps those people will move into the flats that are built here. Then that block of streets can be knocked down.'

'There's the fiddle again!' said Roland. It was distant, as before, and fierce. 'But I can't see the old man. Where is he?'

'What's the matter with you today, Roland? Stop dithering: he'll be somewhere around.'

'Yes, but where? He was by the lamp post a second ago, and it's miles to the houses. We couldn't hear him and not see him.'

'I'd rather know where Helen and David have got to,' said Nicholas. 'If they don't hurry up the gang'll be back before we've found the ball.'

'Do you think they're all right –?'

'Of course they are. They're trying to have us on.'

'They may be stuck, or locked in,' said Roland.

'They'd have shouted,' said Nicholas. 'No: they're up to something. You wait here, in case they try to sneak out. I'm going to surprise them.'

Roland sat down on a broken kitchen chair that was a part of the landscape. He was cold.

Then the music came again.

Roland jumped up, but there was no fiddler in sight, and he could not make out which direction the sound was coming from.

'Nick?'

The music faded.

'Nick! – Nick!'

The wasteland was bigger in the late afternoon light; the air quiet; and the houses seemed to be painted in the dusk. They were as alien as a coastline from the sea. A long way off, a woman pushed a pram.

'Nick!'

Roland picked his way over the rubble to the other side of the church, and here he found a door which sagged open on broken hinges: two floorboards were nailed across the doorway. Roland climbed through into a passage with several small rooms leading off it. Water trickled from a fractured pipe. There were the smells of soot and cat.

The rooms were empty except for the things that are always left behind. There were some mouldering Sunday school registers; a brass-bound Bible; a faded sepia photograph of the Whitsun procession of 1909; a copy of Kirton's Standard Temperance Reciter, Presented to John Beddowes by the Pendlebury Band of Hope, February 1888. There was a broken saucer. There was a jam jar furred green with long-dried water.

'Nick!'

Roland went through into the body of the church.

The floorboards and joists had been taken way, leaving the bare earth: everything movable had been ripped out down to the brick. The church was a cavern. Above Roland's head the three lancets of the west window glowed like orange candles against the fading light. The middle lancet, the tallest, was shattered, and the glass lay on the earth. But there was no ball.

'Nick! Helen! David! Where are you?'

The dusk hung like mist in the church.

Roland went back to the passage. At the end was a staircase. The banisters had been pulled out, but the steps remained.

'David! Nick! Come down: please don't hide! I don't like it!'

No one answered. Roland's footsteps thumped on the stairs. Two rooms opened off a landing at the top, and both were empty.

'Nick!'

The echo filled the church.

'Nick!'

Round, and round, his voice went, and through it came a noise. It was low and vibrant, like wind in a chimney. It grew louder, more taut, and the wall blurred, and the floor shook. The noise was in the fabric of the church: it pulsed with sound. Then he heard a heavy door open; and close; and the noise faded away. It was now too still in the church, and footsteps were moving over the rubble in the passage downstairs.

'Who's that?' said Roland.

The footsteps reached the stair, and began to climb.

'Who's there?'

'Do not be afraid,' said a voice.

'Who are you? What do you want?'

The footsteps were at the top of the stairs. A shadow fell across the landing.

'No!' cried Roland. 'Don't come any nearer!'

The fiddler stood in the doorway.

'I shall not harm you. Take the end of my bow, and lead me. The stairs are dangerous.'

He was bent, and thin: he limped: his voice was old: there looked to be no strength in him: and he was between Roland and the stairs. He stretched out his fiddle bow.

'Help me.'

'All – all right.'

Roland put his hand forward to take the bow, but as he was about to touch it a shock struck his finger tips, driving light through his forehead between his eyes. It was as though a shutter had been lifted in his mind, and in the moment before it dropped again he saw something; but it went so quickly that all he could hold was the shape of its emptiness.

'What did you see?'

'See? I didn't – see. I – through my fingers – see? Towers – like flame. – A candle in darkness. – A black wind.'

'Lead me.'

'Yes.'

Roland went down the stairs, a step at a time, dazed but no longer frightened. The church was somehow remote from him now, and flat, like a piece of stage scenery. The only real things were the fiddler and his bow.

'I heard your music,' said Roland. 'Why were you playing so far away from people?'

'I was near you. Are you not people?' They had reached the bottom of the stairs, and were standing on the earth floor of the church. 'Give me my bow.'

'I can't stay,' said Roland. But the old man put the fiddle to his shoulder. 'I'm looking for my sister, and my two brothers –' The old man began to play. '– and I must find them before dark –' It was the wild dance. '– and we've a train to catch. What's that noise? – Please! – Stop! – It's hurting! – Please! –'

The air took up the fiddler's note. It was the sound Roland had heard upstairs, but now it was louder, building waves that jarred the church, and went through Roland's body until he felt that he was threaded on the sound.

'– Please! –'

'Now! Open the door!'

'I can't! It's locked!'

'Open it! There is little time!'

'But –!'

'Now!'

Roland stumbled to the door, grasped the iron handle, and pulled with all his weight. The door opened, and he ran out on to the cobbles of the street, head down, driven by the noise.

But he never reached the far pavement, for the cobbles were moving under him. He turned. The outline of the church rippled in the air, and vanished. He was standing among boulders on a sea shore, and the music died into the crash of breakers, and the long fall of surf.

Elidor
Alan Garner

Earth Orbit As she let herself in through the back gate which had a wooden latch to keep the cows out of the garden, she caught sight of Brian. He was still playing with the glass float in the sand-heap beside the wash-house.

'Don't forget you're doing the ducks and fowls tonight. You promised.'

He looked up at her vaguely, his hands busy with some

complicated design in the sand.

'All right, Zel, I won't forget.' Why was she always worrying about time, just like a grown-up? 'Time to wash your hands for tea, time for school, time to feed the ducks. . . .' Just when he was in the middle of something really important; like guiding a spaceship in orbit around the Earth. He dismissed her with a frown and bent over the controls again. As he steered the ship, he kept his eyes fixed on the smoky green globe of Earth gleaming in the sunlight far below.

If you slitted up your eyes, you could make out the shapes of the continents. Those bulges joined by the thin stain of land near the equator were North and South America, and that shape like an upside-down pear was Africa. If you tried hard enough, you could see even the tiny thrusting shapes of the North and South Islands as you hurtled along at fifteen thousand miles an hour.

Yet somehow it was hard to see the British Isles. Maybe it was the fog which lay over that part of the world where the Gulf Stream meets the cold current, or perhaps his orbit was taking him too far below the equator. . . . He could see Asia and the scatter of islands that was Japan. If he strained really hard, screwing up his eyes, he fancied he could even see some of the big cities – but he was not sure.

Events on Earth seemed so petty and unimportant to Brian that he did not hear his mother calling him until her voice began to rise on the last syllable of his name. Through his observation window, he noticed that she had caught sight of him from the back verandah.

'Go and see to those fowls, this instant!'

'Yes, Mum.'

He plunged back into the heavy atmosphere of the earth and landed in a desert. Perhaps on Mars or Venus, or on some other planet in another galaxy, there were machines that laid eggs without needing fuel?

When he had scattered the wheat and put the old saucepan back on the shelf above the feed drum, he ran back to the sand-heap, but the beautiful, smoky-green globe of the earth had vanished. All that was left were a concave dimple and the curving trails in the grey waste where his space-ship had orbited.

A Walk on the Beach
O. E. Middleton

I Dreamed I Was

Oh I dreamed I was walking alone,
In a city of sadness,
And I wandered thro' deserts of stone,
In a jungle of drabness.
I saw children in rows were reciting the rules,
And the railings were high that surrounded the schools,
And I knew that it wasn't a dream,
Slabs of stone where the grass should have been.

And the walls were a wilderness high,
And the sun was in hiding,
And the towers were tearing the sky,
Where the smoke clouds were writhing,
And the God of the city had iron jaws,
A ragged monster with jagged claws,
And I knew that it wasn't a dream,
Smoke and dust where the heart should have been.

In the markets where daydreams were sold,
The blind men were masters,
Turning all that they touched into gold,
The blind men were masters.
I saw a million doorways and a million rooms,
A million mourners and a million tombs,
And I knew it wasn't a dream,
A million masks where the faces should have been.

Then at last the sun shone in my dream,
And toppled each tower,
There where the stone slabs had been,
The earth was in flower.
And the iron bars melted everyone,
The stone walls quivered and cracked in the sun,
And I saw that it couldn't have been,
And I knew it was only a dream.

Leon Rosselson

The Loch Ness Monster's Song

Sssnnnwhufffll?
Hnwhuffl hhnnwfl hnfl hfl?
Gdroblboblhobngbl gbl gl g g g g glbgl.
Drublhaflablhaflubhafgabhaflhafl fl fl —
gm grawwwww grf grawf awfgm graw gin.
Hovoplodok-doplodovok-plovodokot-doplodokosh?
Splgraw fok fok splgrafhatchgabrlgabrl fok splfok!
Zgra kra gka fok!
Grof grawff gahf?
Gombl mbl bl —
blm plm,
blm plm,
blm plm,
blp.

Edwin Morgan

Tyrannosaurus Rex

It came on great oiled, resilient, striding, legs. It towered thirty feet above half of the trees, a great evil god, folding its delicate watchmaker's claws close to its oily reptilian chest. Each lower leg was a piston, a thousand pounds of white bone, sunk in thick ropes of muscle, sheathed over in a gleam of pebbled skin like the mail of a terrible warrior. Each thigh was a ton of meat, ivory and steel mesh. And from that great breathing cage of the upper body those two delicate arms dangled out front, arms with hands which might pick up and examine men like toys, while the snake neck coiled. And the head itself, a ton of sculptured stone, lifted easily upon the sky. Its mouth gaped, exposing a fence of teeth like daggers. Its eyes rolled, ostrich eggs, empty of all expression save hunger. It closed its mouth in a death grin. It ran, its pelvic bones crushing aside trees and bushes, its taloned feet clawing damp earth, leaving prints six inches deep wherever it settled its weight. It ran with a gliding ballet step, far too poised and balanced for its ten tons. It moved into a sunlit arena warily, its beautifully reptile hands feeling the air.

Ray Bradbury

The One Who Waits

I live in a well. I live like smoke in the well. Like vapour in a stone throat. I don't move. I don't do anything but wait. Overhead I see the cold stars of night and morning, and I see the sun. And sometimes I sing old songs of this world when it was young. How can I tell you what I am when I don't know? I cannot. I am simply waiting. I am mist and moonlight and memory. I am sad and I am old. Sometimes I fall like rain into the well. Spider webs are startled into forming where my rain falls fast, on the water surface. I wait in cool silence and there will be a day when I no longer wait.

Now it is morning. I hear a great thunder. I smell fire from a distance. I hear a metal crashing. I wait. I listen.

Voices. Far away.

'All right!'

One voice. An alien voice. An alien tongue I cannot know. No word is familiar. I listen.

'Send the men out!'

A crunching in crystal sands.

'Mars! So this is it!'

'Where's the flag?'

'Here, sir.'

'Good, good.'

The sun is high in the blue sky and its golden rays fill the well and I hang like a flower pollen, invisible and misting in the warm light.

Voices.

'In the name of the Government of Earth, I proclaim this to be the Martian Territory, to be equally divided among the member nations.'

What are they saying? I turn in the sun, like a wheel, invisible and lazy, golden and tireless.

'What's over here?'

'A well!'

'No!'

'Come on. Yes!'

The approach of warmth. Three objects bend over the well mouth, and my coolness rises to the object.

'Great!'

'Think it's good water?'

'We'll see.'

'Someone get a lab test bottle and a dropline.'

'I will!'

A sound of running. The return.

'Here we are.'

I wait.

'Let it down. Easy.'

Glass shines, above, coming down on a slow line.

The water ripples softly as the glass touches and fills. I rise in the warm air toward the well mouth.

'Here we are. You want to test this water, Regent?'

'Let's have it.'

'What a beautiful well. Look at that construction. How old do you think it is?'

'God knows. When we landed in that other town yesterday Smith said there hasn't been life on Mars in ten thousand years.'

'Imagine.'

'How is it, Regent? The water.'

'Pure as silver. Have a glass.'

The sound of water in the hot sunlight. Now I hover like a dust, a cinnamon, upon the soft wind.

'What's the matter, Jones?'

'I don't know. Got a terrible headache. All of a sudden.'

'Did you drink the water yet?'

'No, I haven't. It's not that. I was just bending over the well and all of a sudden my head split. I feel better now.'

Now I know who I am.

My name is Stephen Leonard Jones and I am twenty-five
years old and I have just come in a rocket from a planet called
Earth and I am standing with my good friends Regent and
Shaw by an old well on the planet Mars.

I look down at my golden fingers, tan and strong. I look at my
long legs and at my silver uniform and at my friends.

'What's wrong, Jones?' they say.

'Nothing,' I say, looking at them. 'Nothing at all.'

The food is good. It has been ten thousand years since food. It
touches the tongue in a fine way and the wine with the food is
warming. I listen to the sound of voices. I make words that I do
not understand but somehow understand. I test the air.

'What's the matter, Jones?'

I tilt this head of mine and rest my hands holding the silver
utensils of eating. I feel everything.

'What do you mean?' this voice, this new thing of mine, says.

'You keep breathing funny. Coughing,' says the other man.

I pronounce exactly. 'Maybe a little cold coming on.'

'Check with the doc later.'

I nod my head and it is good to nod. It is good to do several
things after ten thousand years. It is good to breathe the air
and it is good to feel the sun in the flesh deep and going
deeper and it is good to feel the structure of ivory, the fine
skeleton hidden in the warming flesh, and it is good to hear
sounds much clearer and more immediate than they were in
the stone deepness of a well. I sit enchanted.

'Come out of it, Jones. Snap to it. We got to move!'

'Yes,' I say, hypnotized with the way the word forms like
water on the tongue and falls with slow beauty out into the air.

I walk and it is good walking. I stand high and it is a long
way to the ground when I look down from my eyes and my
head. It is like living on a fine cliff and being happy there.

Regent stands by the stone well, looking down. The others
have gone murmuring to the silver ship from which they came.

I feel the fingers of my hand and the smile of my mouth.

'It is deep,' I say.

'Yes.'

'It is called a Soul Well.'

Regent raises his head and looks at me. 'How do you know that?'

'Doesn't it look like one?'

'I never heard of a Soul Well.'

'A place where waiting things, things that once had flesh, wait and wait,' I say, touching his arm.

The sand is fire and the ship is silver fire in the hotness of the day and the heat is good to feel. The sound of my feet in the hard sand. I listen. The sound of the wind and the sun burning the valleys. I smell the smell of the rocket boiling in the noon. I stand below the port.

'Where's Regent?' someone says.

'I saw him by the well,' I reply.

One of them runs towards the well. I am beginning to tremble. A fine shivering tremble, hidden deep, but becoming very strong. And for the first time I hear it, as if it too were hidden in a well. A voice calling deep within me, tiny and afraid. And the voice cries, *Let me go, let me go*, and there is a feeling as if something is trying to get free, a pounding of labyrinthine doors, a rushing down dark corridors and up passages, echoing and screaming.

'Regent's in the well!'

The men are running, all five of them. I run with them but now I am sick and the trembling is violent.

'He must have fallen. Jones, you were here with him. Did you see? Jones? Well, speak up, man.'

'What's wrong, Jones?'

I fall to my knees, the trembling is so bad.

'He's sick. Here, help me with him.'

'The sun.'

'No, not the sun,' I murmur.

They stretch me out and the seizures come and go like earthquakes and the deep hidden voice in me cries, *This is*

Jones, this is me, that's not him, that's not him, don't believe him, let me out, let me out! And I look up at the bent figures and my eyelids flicker. They touch my wrists.

'His heart is acting up.'

I close my eyes. The screaming stops. The shivering ceases.

I rise, as in a cool well, released.

'He's dead,' says someone.

'Jones is dead.'

'From what?'

'Shock, it looks like.'

'What kind of shock?' I say, and my name is Sessions and my lips move crisply, and I am the captain of these men. I stand among them and I am looking down at a body which lies cooling on the sands. I clap both hands to my head.

'Captain!'

'It's nothing,' I say, crying out. 'Just a headache. I'll be all right. There. There,' I whisper. 'It's all right now.'

'We'd better get out of the sun, sir.'

'Yes,' I say, looking down at Jones. 'We should never have come. Mars doesn't want us.'

We carry the body back to the rocket with us, and a new voice is calling deep in me to be let out.

Help, help. Far down in the moist earthen-works of the body. *Help, help!* in red fathoms, echoing and pleading.

The trembling starts much sooner this time. The control is less steady.

'Captain, you'd better get in out of the sun, you don't look too well, sir.'

'Yes,' I say. 'Help,' I say.

'What, sir?'

'I didn't say anything.'

'You said 'Help,' sir.'

'Did I, Matthews, did I?'

The body is laid out in the shadow of the rocket and the voice screams in the deep underwater catacombs of bone and crimson tide. My hands jerk. My mouth splits and is parched. My nostrils fasten wide. My eyes roll. *Help, help, oh help, don't, don't, let me out, don't, don't.*

'Don't,' I say.

'What, sir?'

'Never mind,' I say. 'I've got to get free,' I say. I clap my hand to my mouth.

'How's that, sir?' cries Matthews.

'Get inside, all of you, go back to Earth!' I shout.

A gun in my hand. I lift it.

'Don't, sir!'

An explosion. Shadows run. The screaming is cut off. There is a whistling sound of falling through space.

After ten thousand years, how good to die. How good to feel the sudden coolness, the relaxation. How good to be like a hand within a glove that stretches out and grows wonderfully cold in the hot sand. Oh, the quiet and the loveliness of gathering, darkening death. But one cannot linger on.

A crack, a snap.

'Good God, he's killed himself!' I cry, and open my eyes and there is the captain lying against the rocket, his skull split by a bullet, his eyes wide, his tongue protruding between his white teeth. Blood runs from his head. I bend to him and touch him. 'The fool,' I say. 'Why did he do that?'

The men are horrified. They stand over the two dead men and turn their heads to see the Martian sands and the distant well where Regent lies lolling in deep waters. A croaking comes out of their dry lips, a whimpering, a childish protest against this awful dream.

The men turn to me.

After a long while, one of them says, 'That makes you captain, Matthews.'

'I know,' I say slowly.

'Only six of us left.'

'Good God, it happened so quick!'

'I don't want to stay here, let's get out!'

The men clamour. I go to them and touch them now, with a confidence which almost sings in me. 'Listen,' I say, and touch their elbows or their arms or their hands.

We all fall silent.

We are one.

No, no, no, no, no, no! Inner voices crying, deep down and gone into prisons beneath exteriors.

We are looking at each other. We are Samuel Matthews and Raymond Moses and William Spaulding and Charles Evans and Forrest Cole and John Summers, and we say nothing but look upon each other and our white faces and shaking hands.

We turn, as one, and look at the well.

'Now,' we say.

No, no, six voices scream, hidden and layered down and stored forever.

Our feet walk in the sand and it is as if a great hand with twelve fingers were moving across the hot sea bottom.

We bend to the well, looking down. From the cool depths six faces peer back up at us.

One by one we bend until our balance is gone, and one by one drop into the mouth and down through cool darkness into the cool waters.

The sun sets. The stars wheel upon the night sky. Far out, there is a wink of light. Another rocket coming, leaving red marks on space.

I live in a well. I live like smoke in a well. Like vapour in a stone throat. Overhead I see the cold stars of night and morning, and I see the sun. And sometimes I sing old songs of this world when it was young. How can I tell you what I am when even I don't know? I cannot.

Ray Bradbury I am simply waiting.

Under a Ramshackle Rainbow

A dead tree.
On a rotten branch sit two wingless birds. Among leaves
on the ground a man is searching for his hands.
It is fall.

A stagnant marsh.
On a mossy stone sits the man angling. The hook
is stuck in a waterlily.
The waterlily is stuck in the mud.

An overgrown ruin.
In the grass the man sleeps sitting up. A raindrop descends

in slow-motion through space.
Somewhere in the grass a pike flounders.

A dry well.
At the bottom lies a dead fly. In the wood nearby
a spider gropes through the fog.
The man is trapped in the spiderweb on the horizon.

*Translated from the
Swedish by May
Swenson*
Ingemar Gustafson
An abandoned ant hill.
Above a little woodmarsh floats the man. The sun
is just going down. The man has already stopped growing.
The ants gather on the shore.

Gnaw short the long nose

Thomas Lovell Beddoes

Gnaw short the long nose,
  Gnaw, quoth the short.
Which is the wrong nose
  When both snort?

Resurrection Song

Thread the nerves through the right holes,
Get out of my bones, you wormy souls.
Shut up my stomach, the ribs are full:
Muscles be steady and ready to pull.
Heart and artery merrily shake
And eyelid go up, for we're ready to wake. –

Thomas Lovell Beddoes

His eye must be brighter – one more rub!
And pull up the nostrils! his nose was snub.

The Legend of Alderley

At dawn one still October day in the long ago of the world, across the hill of Alderley, a farmer from Mobberley was riding to Macclesfield fair.

The morning was dull, but mild; light mists bedimmed his way; the woods were hushed; the day promised fine. The farmer was in good spirits, and he let his horse, a milk-white mare, set her own pace, for he wanted her to arrive fresh for the market. A rich man would go back to Mobberley that night.

So, his mind in the town while he was yet on the hill, the farmer drew near to the place known as Thieves' Hole. And there the horse stood still and would answer to neither spur nor rein. The spur and the rein she understood, and her master's stern command, but the eyes that held her were stronger than all of these.

In the middle of the path, where surely there had been no one, was an old man, tall, with long hair and beard. 'You go to sell this mare,' he said. 'I come here to buy. What is your price?'

But the farmer wished to sell only at the market, where he would have the choice of many offers, so he rudely bade the stranger quit the path and let him through, for if he stayed longer he would be late to the fair.

'Then go your way,' said the old man. 'None will buy. And I shall await you here at sunset.'

The next moment he was gone, and the farmer could not tell how or where.

The day was warm, and the tavern cool, and all who saw the mare agreed that she was a splendid animal, the pride of Cheshire, a queen among horses; and everyone said that there was no finer beast in the town that day. But no one offered to buy. A weary, sour-eyed farmer rode up out of Macclesfield as the sky reddened the west.

At Thieves' Hole the mare would not budge: the stranger was there.

Thinking any price now better than none, the farmer agreed to sell. 'How much will you give?' he said.

'Enough. Now come with me.'

By Seven Firs and Golderstone they went, to Stormy Point and Saddlebole. And they halted before a great rock embedded in the hillside. The old man lifted his staff and lightly touched the rock, and it split with the noise of thunder.

At this, the farmer toppled from his plunging horse, and, on his knees, begged the other to have mercy on him and let him go on his way unharmed. The horse should stay; he did not want her. Only spare his life, that was enough.

The wizard, for such he was, commanded the farmer to rise. 'I promise you safe conduct,' he said. 'Do not be afraid; for living wonders you shall see here'.

Beyond the rock stood a pair of iron gates. These the wizard opened, and took the farmer and his horse down a narrow tunnel deep into the hill. A light, subdued but beautiful, marked their way. The passage ended, and they stepped into a cave, and there a wondrous sight met the farmer's eyes – a hundred and forty knights in silver armour, and by the side of all but one a milk-white mare.

'Here they lie in enchanted sleep,' said the wizard, 'until a day will come – and come it will – when England shall be in direst peril, and England's mothers weep. Then out from the hill these must ride and, in a battle thrice lost, thrice won, upon the plain, drive the enemy into the sea.'

The farmer, dumb with awe, turned with the wizard into a further cavern, and here mounds of gold and silver and precious stones lay strewn along the ground.

'Take what you can carry in payment for the horse.'

And when the farmer had crammed his pockets (ample as his lands!), his shirt and his fists with jewels, the wizard hurried him up the long tunnel and thrust him out of the gates. The farmer stumbled, the thunder rolled, he looked, and there was only the bare rock face above him. He was alone on the hill, near Stormy Point. The broad full moon was up, and it was night.

The Weirdstone of
Brisingamen
Alan Garner

And although in later years he tried to find the place, neither he nor any after him ever saw the iron gates again.

Death a Prisoner   This happened many hundreds of years ago.

In those far off days, in the Valais in Switzerland, the sun was so hot, and fertile rains fell in such abundance, that the peasants could plant grapevines right up to the edge of the eternal glaciers. With the grapes they could make a potent and fragrant wine which they called glacier milk.

But there were bad harvests even in those days. One year there was no rain; the leaves of the vines turned yellowish and then brown. The grapes shrivelled up till there was nothing left of them.

High up on the mountainside lived a wine grower, whose many huge wine barrels were filled every year after the vintage. But in this bad year the few grapes he managed to harvest hardly yielded enough wine to fill one tiny little cask.

'This wine is not going to be kept,' cried the farmer in his vexation and disappointment; 'it isn't worth it. I shall take it out on the road, and the first person who comes along shall help me drink it.'

At that he hoisted the little cask, with the wine gurgling inside, on to his shoulder, and set out for the next village. On the road he met a traveller of noble bearing, walking along with easy strides. 'Hi, stranger!' he cried to him, 'will you help me to drink this year's vintage? There is so little that it is not worth keeping.'

The stranger agreed. The two sat down together by the roadside, and as the wine grower handed the cask to the unknown traveller, inviting him to drink from it, he asked who his drinking companion might be. 'I am the Lord God,' came the answer. At that the wine grower pulled the little cask back with a jerk. 'What!' he shouted, 'you are the Lord God? Then I shan't give you any wine. What have you been about this year? What have you been doing with the weather? The grapes, the corn, the grass, everything has dried up. Go your way! I am not going to share my wine with you.'

The Lord God went on his way, and the wine grower looked about him for another drinking companion. Soon he saw a thin bony little man coming up the road. He stopped him and spoke to him, suggesting that they should empty the cask together. The stranger did not wait to be asked twice. And when the wine grower asked him where he was going to, and where he came from, he answered, 'I am Death.'

'Oh, you are Death!' said the wine grower, and a shiver ran down his back. 'What have you come here for?'

'I have come to fetch your neighbour,' answered Death.

'My neighbour?' laughed the wine grower, 'then you've come in vain. It's true he is ill, but all his men are out in the fields, and they have bolted the door of his house carefully. You won't get in.'

'Oh!' said Death, 'I can get in anywhere. Where the tiniest mote in a sunbeam can get in, I can get in too.'

The wine grower grew thoughtful. He was fond of his neighbour. Suddenly an almost imperceptible smile flitted over his face. Again and again he handed Death the cask and invited him to drink. 'I don't believe you,' he said at last firmly, 'when you say you can get in anywhere. You couldn't even squeeze yourself through the bung-hole of my cask, let alone through the thin cracks which let in the motes of sunlight.'

Death had done the wine full justice. And now he thought to himself, no peasant should say that he was not as good as his word, or that he had pretended to powers that he had not got. He screwed himself up into a tiny ball, and dived head first into the little cask through the bung-hole. As soon as he was inside, the wine grower seized the cork, stopped up the bung-hole, with it and then hammered it home with a heavy stone. Now Death was a prisoner. The man took up the cask, carried it home and down into his cellar, and there he threw it into the farthest and darkest corner, where no one set foot for years at a time.

And because Death was imprisoned, nobody could die in the Valais. Little children came into the world, they grew up, grew old, became fathers and grandfathers, but their own fathers and grandfathers were still alive. The valley became too small for this rich crop of humanity, and many migrated southwards, down to the sea.

In the evenings, when the very old folk were sitting together, and longing for death, because they felt that the young folk did not understand them, one or other would speak of the good old times when it was possible to die, and they all hoped ardently that Death would one day take up his work again.

The wine grower who had taken Death prisoner belonged to this company of the very old. He had long ago forgotten his meeting with Death, and like all the others longed to be able to die. He was aged and embittered. His grandchildren and great-grandchildren would not listen to the advice he gave them.

In this state of melancholy he went down one day into his cellar, in order to seek the comfort of a drop of wine. He felt his way past the big wine barrels, farther and farther towards the back of the vault, and came at last to the little cask which he had thrown there so many decades ago.

He shook it and it gurgled softly. 'That must be a good old wine,' he said to himself, removing the tightly-jammed cork with some difficulty. Suddenly the prisoner sprang out, leapt at his throat and strangled him to death.

And now a terrible dying spread over the district. Death attacked his victims like a starving man, here one or two, there a dozen, here a whole family, there half a village. He was making up for the idleness of hundreds of years. Farms went to rack and ruin, whole hamlets and villages were deserted. The survivors on the mountainsides decided to band themselves together into one community, and to establish themselves down below in the valley. And because the mountain ridges and slopes were no longer cultivated by diligent hands, the fruitful fields, vineyards and farms turned into wilderness. Today the mountainside above the valley is nothing but a stony desert.

Translated from the German by K. Potts
Fritz Müller-Guggenbühl

The Fight   Gliding through the shadows came
the walker in the night; the warriors slept
whose task was to hold the horned building,
all except one. It was well-known to men
that the demon could not drag them to the shades
without God's willing it; yet the one man kept
unblinking watch. He awaited, heart swelling
with anger against his foe, the ordeal of battle.

Down off the moorlands' misting fells came
Grendel stalking; God's brand was on him.
The spoiler meant to snatch away
from the high hall some of human race.
He came on under the clouds, clearly saw at last
the gold-hall of men, the mead-drinking place
nailed with gold plates. That was not the first visit
he had paid to the hall of Hrothgar the Dane:
he never before and never after
harder luck nor hall-guards found.

Walking to the hall came this warlike creature
condemned to agony. The door gave way,
toughened with iron, at the touch of those hands.
Rage-inflamed, wreckage-bent, he ripped open
the jaws of the hall. Hastening on,
the foe then stepped onto the unstained floor,
angrily advanced: out of his eyes stood
an unlovely light like that of fire.
He saw then in the hall a host of young soldiers,
a company of kinsmen caught away in sleep,
a whole warrior band. In his heart he laughed then,
horrible monster, his hopes swelling
to a gluttonous meal. He meant to wrench
the life from each body that lay in the place
before night was done. (It was not to be;
he was no longer to feast on the flesh of mankind
after that night.)
                              Narrowly the powerful
kinsman of Hygelac kept watch how the ravager
set to work with his sudden catches;
nor did the monster mean to hang back.
As a first step he set his hands on
a sleeping soldier, savagely tore at him,
gnashed at his bone-joints, bolted huge gobbets,
sucked at his veins, and had soon eaten

all of the dead man, even down to his
hands and feet.
                           Forward he stepped,
stretched out his hands to attach that warrior
calmly at rest there, reached out for him with his
unfriendly fingers: but the faster man
forestalling, sat up, sent back his arm.
The upholder of evils at once knew
he had not met, on middle earth's
extremest acres, with any man
of harder hand-grip: his heart panicked.
(He was quit of the place no more quickly for that.)
Eager to be away, he ailed for his darkness
and the company of devils; the dealings he had there
were like nothing he had come across in his lifetime.

Then Hygelac's brave kinsman called to mind
that evening's utterance, upright he stood,
fastened his hold till fingers were bursting.
The monster strained away: the man stepped closer.
The famed one's desire was for darkness between them,
direction regardless, to get out and run
for his fen-bordered lair; he felt his grip's strength
crushed by his enemy. It was an ill journey
the rough marauder had made to Heorot.

The crash in the banqueting-hall came to the Danes,
the men of the guard that remained in the building,
as a taste of death. The deepening rage
of the claimants to Heorot caused it to resound.
It was indeed wonderful that the wine-supper-hall
withstood the wrestling pair, that the world's palace
fell not to the ground. But it was girt firmly,
both inside and out, by iron braces
of skilled manufacture. Many a figured
gold-worked wine-bench, as we have heard,
started from the floor at the struggles of that pair.
The men of the Danes had not imagined that
any of mankind by what method soever
might undo that intricate, antlered hall,
sunder it by strength, unless it were swallowed up in
the embraces of fire.
                           Fear entered into
the listening North Danes, as that noise rose up again
strange and strident. It shrilled terror

to the ears that heard it through the hall's side-wall,
the grisly plaint of God's enemy,
his song of ill-success, the sobs of the damned one
bewailing his pain. He was pinioned there
by the man of all mankind living
in this world's estate the strongest of his hands.

Not for anything would the earls' guardian
let his deadly guest go living:
he did not count his continued existence
of the least use to anyone. The earls ran
to defend the person of their famous prince;
they drew their ancestral swords to bring
what aid they could to their captain, Beowulf.
They were ignorant of this – when they entered the fight,
boldly-intentioned battle-friends,
to hew at Grendel, hunt his life
on every side – that no sword on earth,
not the truest steel, could touch their assailant;
for by a spell he had dispossessed all
blades of their bite against him.
                                    A bitter parting
from life was that day destined for him;

weird   the eldritch spirit was sent off on his
far faring into the fiends' domain.

It was then that this monster, who, moved by spite
against human kind, had caused so much harm
in his feud with God found at last
that flesh and bone were to fail him in the end;
for Hygelac's great-hearted kinsman
had him by the hand; and hateful to each
was the breath of the other.
                                    A breach in the giant
flesh-frame showed then, shoulder-muscles
sprang apart, there was a snapping of tendons,
bone-locks burst. To Beowulf the glory
of this fight was granted; Grendel's lot
to flee the slopes fen-ward with flagging heart,
to a den where he knew there could be no relief,
no refuge for a life at its very last stage,
whose surrender-day had dawned. The Danish hopes
in this fatal fight had found their answer.

He had cleansed Heorot! He who had come from afar,
deep-minded, strong-hearted, had saved the hall

from persecution. He was pleased with his night's work,
the deed he had done. Before the Danish people
the Great captain had made good his boast,
had taken away all their unhappiness,
the evil menace under which they had lived,
enduring it by dire constraint,
no slight affliction. As a signal to all
the hero hung up the hand, the arm
and torn-off shoulder, the entire limb,
Grendel's whole grip, below the gable of the roof.

Translated from the
Anglo-Saxon by
Michael Alexander
Anonymous

Wodwo

What am I? Nosing here, turning leaves over
Following a faint stain on the air to the river's edge
I enter water. What am I to split
The glassy grain of water looking upward I see the bed
of the river above me upside down very clear
What am I doing here in mid-air? Why do I find
this frog so interesting as I inspect its most secret
interior and make it my own? Do these weeds
know me and name me to each other have they
seen me before, do I fit in their world? I seem
separate from the ground and not rooted but dropped
out of nothing casually I've no threads
fastening me to anything I can go anywhere
I seem to have been given freedom
Of this place what am I then? And picking
bits of bark off this rotten stump gives me
no pleasure and it's no use so why do I do it
me and doing that have coincided very queerly
But what shall I be called am I the first
have I an owner what shape am I what
shape am I am I huge if I go
to the end of this way past these trees and past these trees
till I get tired that's touching one wall of me
for the moment if I sit still how everything
stops to watch me I suppose I am the exact centre
but there's all this what is it roots
roots roots roots and here's the water
Ted Hughes again very queer but I'll go on looking

Heartless Beauty The young queen, Lustrous Tortoiseshell, wife of the last king of the house of Chou, had eyes the colour of topaz. Her skin was as smooth as her petticoat of apricot-yellow satin, and when she yawned she showed the inside of a mouth coral and crinkled as a cat's. She yawned often, for she found life in the palace remarkably tedious. Indeed the king was a dull, gloomy man, whose courtiers would hide their smiles behind their wide sleeves when they saw him coming, for fear of incurring his displeasure.

It was not altogether the king's fault. Ever since he had ascended the Dragon Throne, the borders of China had been menaced by enemy horsemen, and every day he was forced to spend long hours in council with his ministers discussing their defence, until his forehead was furrowed with care. But Lustrous Tortoiseshell did not understand this, and instead of seeking humbly to please her lord, or to distract his mind from care – which all the ancient writings agree is the first duty of a wife – she preferred to sulk in her own apartments. Bored, she tore up pieces of valuable silk, her eyes glinting with pleasure at the sound. The rasp of rending embroideries set the king's teeth on edge, and made him gloomier than ever.

'Lustrous Tortoiseshell,' he implored her, 'the King of Chou is your slave, but he begs you humbly not to tear any more silk.'

For answer the queen only yawned and tapped impatiently with her little foot upon the floor. The king sent for jugglers, lute players and dancing bears; he ordered merchants to bring their most precious wares of jade and ivory and chiselled gold, yet still this spoilt beauty continued to frown. He was in despair to know how to please her.

At last one day, when Lustrous Tortoiseshell had sat sulking for two hours without a smile, the king had an idea. He gathered up his long robe, took a lighted taper in his hand, and climbed the winding stair to the highest watchtower of the palace, where a sentry stood night and day, looking out over the plain. There upon the floor a great fire was prepared; brushwood, pine cones and logs of cedarwood, all ready to flare up at a touch. It was the beacon to give warning that the enemy was at hand. Into this beacon the king thrust his lighted taper.

There was a rustle among the twigs, a sudden roar and flames leapt like a fountain into the air. Soon, almost at once it seemed, came an answering roar from the distance. It was the sound of many hands beating on bronze war drums, as the faithful nobles of Chou led their troops out of their castles to defend the king. Winding down the valleys they came, from each castle an army of men, on horse, on foot, with banners streaming in the wind, forests of lances glittering in the sunshine and chariots swaying from side to side in their headlong advance.

Lustrous Tortoiseshell, all boredom forgotten, watched from her window as the armies met and poured in like a mighty river at the city gate. They crowded into the courtyard of the palace, jostling for position and shouting their battle cries. Some of the foot-soldiers, in the belief that the enemy was at hand, began to throw their firecrackers without waiting for orders, and so terrified the horses that several onlookers were trampled to death.

The chief nobles of Chou rode forward to the palace doors upon their foaming chargers. They were accoutred for war, their supple leather riding boots pulled up to their thighs, their well-flighted arrows in quivers at their sides, the visors of their bronze helmets, grim and terrible, pulled over their eyes. They reined in their horses and waited silently at the palace steps for their king to come out and lead them.

But the King of Chou was too ashamed to show his face. In an inner courtyard of the palace he gave himself over to despair.

'Honoured sirs, honoured sirs,' called Lustrous Tortoiseshell from the window 'you may all go home to your castles of exalted virtue, and there employ the remainder of your days peacefully flying kites. The enemy is not here.'

'Not here?'

'Not here?'

Spurs and bridle bells clashed together as the nobles turned to look at each other.

'But the beacon?'

'We saw the beacon flames.'

'The Son of Heaven called us to defend him.'

'His Majesty was pleased to jest with you,' said Lustrous Tortoiseshell.

Silently, without a reproach, so great was their love and loyalty, the nobles turned away. But Lustrous Tortoiseshell, when she saw their amazement, their sorrowful looks and all their warlike trappings hanging useless at their sides, began to laugh.

She flung back her head, closed her eyes to a cat-like slit and laughed for joy, until the last soldier, weary and crestfallen, had left the city gates on his homeward journey. Then she went to the king.

'At last, O King of Chou,' she cried, 'at last you have found means to amuse your wife! How foolish their faces looked when they found there was no enemy! Oh my husband, what a splendid pastime you have invented!'

Shame struck the King of Chou afresh at these words of an idle and worthless woman. At the council table he could hardly bear to meet the grave looks of his ministers, and he vowed that he would never deceive his faithful lords again. But the weeks passed and Lustrous Tortoiseshell grew bored once more. She wheedled and cajoled the unhappy king, she tormented him with her caprices, until in despair he set fire once again to the beacon.

This time the nobles of Chou obeyed the summons with dark looks, and when they saw there was no enemy, departed murmuring that even the king ought not so to make fools of them. When this unwise ruler lit the beacon yet a third time, the nobles chose one, the oldest and most honourable of their numbers, to plead with him. The aged lord, white haired and venerable, prostrated himself humbly upon the steps to the throne.

'Son of Heaven, ruler of earth and sea,' he said. 'Hear, we pray you, the petition of your servants. We know your every thought is for your people's good. Nevertheless there are, around the Dragon Throne, evil counsellors, whose actions, if you but knew of them, your Majesty would never permit. It would be well, O Son of Heaven, if these persons were sent into some distant and unwholesome province. For upon the honour of our ancestors, we nobles of Chou will not be mocked again.'

'I give you my royal word,' said the king, 'that I will never again light the beacon to mock you. Go in peace.' And, laden with rich gifts, he sent them to their homes.

The very next day, as the king and Lustrous Tortoiseshell sat at rice, the watcher on the tower came running down the winding stair and flung himself in terror at their feet.

'Son of Heaven, the enemy is coming!' he cried.

'Where?' said the king, thrusting the golden goblet from his hand.

'Down the mountainsides, through the valleys – their grey cloaks are sweeping like mist over the plains!'

'Let the beacon be lit!' commanded the king. 'Have no fear, my beautiful Lustrous Tortoiseshell, my nobles will bring their armies to defend me.'

But although they fed the beacon fire until its flames leapt as a tall tree, although they beat the bronze war drums and all the temple gongs, yet the nobles did not come. They remembered the laughter of Lustrous Tortoiseshell and feared to be mocked once more.

Then the King of Chou saw – but too late – where his weakness and folly had brought him. As the thunder of enemy horse-hooves sounded nearer and nearer across the plain, he took Lustrous Tortoiseshell by the hand and led her to the tower. When they were both inside he commanded his servents to lock the doors and heap brushwood all around. With his own hands he set fire to the silken hangings. As the first barbarian entered the city gates the king and Lustrous Tortoiseshell perished, both together, in the flames.

So ended the House of Chou.

Translated from the Chinese by Robert Gittings and Jo Manton
Traditional

Nothing is gained, all is lost
Where Heartless Beauty lives.
The man who marries one of these
Has witnessed his own death warrant.

To Make a Play
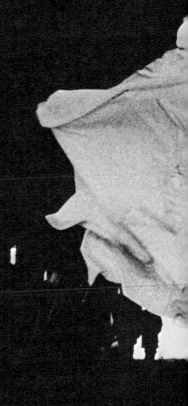

To make a play
is to make people,
to make people do
what you say;

to make real people
do and say
what you make;
to make people make

what you say real;
to make real
people make up
and do what you

make up. What you
make makes people
come and see
what people do

and say, and then
go away and do
what they see –
and see what

they do. Real
people do and say,
and you see and
make up people;

people come to see
what you do.
They see what *they*
do, and they

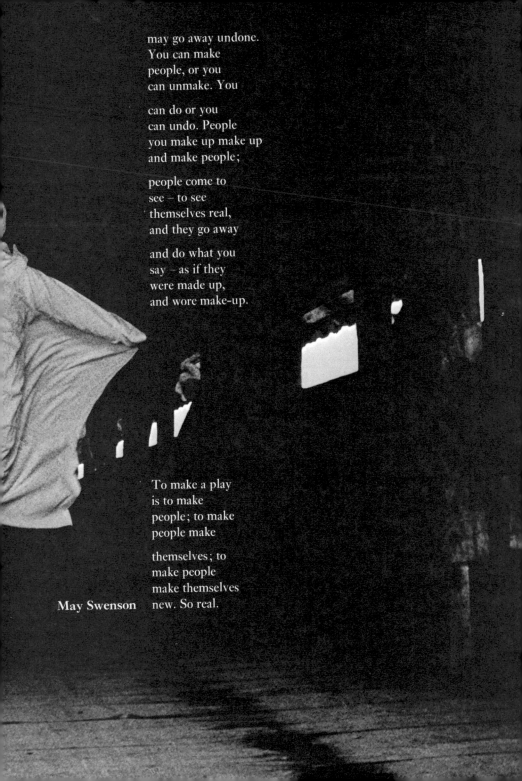

may go away undone.
You can make
people, or you
can unmake. You

can do or you
can undo. People
you make up make up
and make people;

people come to
see – to see
themselves real,
and they go away

and do what you
say – as if they
were made up,
and wore make-up.

To make a play
is to make
people; to make
people make

themselves; to
make people
make themselves
May Swenson new. So real.

Answers to Riddles

Acknowledgements   For permission to use copyright material acknowledgement is made to the following:

Poems and Prose   For 'The Fight' translated by Michael Alexander to the translator; for 'Tyrannosaurus Rex' from 'A Sound of Thunder' and for 'The One Who Waits' from *The Golden Apples of the Sun* by Ray Bradbury to A. D. Peters & Co.; for 'The Making of the Drum' from *Masks* by Edward Brathwaite to the Oxford University Press; for 'The Anchor' from 'The Riddles' translated from the Anglo-Saxon by Kevin Crossley-Holland; for 'Mr Beale' from *All Men Are Islands* by Ronald Duncan to Rupert Hart-Davis Ltd; for 'The Old Blind Fiddler' from 'Thursday's Child' in *Elidor* and 'The Legend of Alderley' in *The Weirdstone of Brisingamen* by Alan Garner to Collins Sons & Co. Ltd; for 'Heartless Beauty' from *The Peachblossom Forest* translated by Robert Gittings and Jo Manton to the translators; for 'The Far Famed Fairy Tale of Fenella' and 'Sale by Auction of the Furniture and Effects of Hookey Walker Esq.' from *Curiosities of Street Literature* to John Foreman, Broadsheet King; for 'The Making of a Monster' from *Loser Weepers* edited by George Hitchcock to the editor; for 'Problems' by Heather Holden from *The Liverpool Scene* edited by Edward Lucie-Smith to the author; for 'Fairy Tale' by Miroslav Holub translated by Ian Milner from *Selected Poems* to Penguin Books Ltd; for 'Foxgloves' from *The Earth-Owl* and 'Wodwo' from *Wodwo* by Ted Hughes to Faber & Faber Ltd; for 'Ye Tortures' from *The Pot-Boiler* by Spike Milligan to the author and Tandem Books; for 'Earth Orbit' from *A Walk on the Beach* by O. E. Middleton to David Higham Associates Ltd; for 'Questions' by Vivian Tuft and Fontessa Moore from *Wishes, Lies and Dreams* by Kenneth Koch to Random House Inc.; for 'The Loch Ness Monster's Song' from *Twelve Songs* by Edwin Morgan to the author and Castlelaw Press; for 'Scariboo' by Christian Morgenstern from *Gallows Song* translated by Max Knight to the University of California Press; for 'Death a Prisoner' from *Swiss-Alpine Folk Tales* by Fritz Müller-Guggenbühl to the Oxford University Press; for 'Sounds' from *Ounce, Dice, Trice* by Alastair Reid to Laurence Pollinger Ltd; for 'I Dreamed I Was' by Leon Rosselson to Harmony Music Ltd; for 'They Have Yarns' from *The People, Yes* by Carl Sandburg to Harcourt Brace Jovanovich Inc.; for 'Cardinal Ideograms', 'The Secret in the Cat' and 'To Make a Play' and for 'Locked In' and 'Under a Ramshackle Rainbow' by Ingemar Gustafson from *Half Sun, Half Sleep* by May Swenson to Charles Scribner's & Sons; for 'Moon People' from *Lucian* translated by Paul Turner to Penguin Books Ltd.

Pictures   For the picture on pages 2-3 to Richard Davies; page 8 to Roger Canessa; pages 10-11 to Cordier and Ekstrom Inc.; pages 14-17 to Atlantic Little, Brown; page 19 to André Deutsch; page 20 to Victoria Brill; page 23 to Hamish Hamilton Ltd; pages 26-7 to John Freeman; page 33 to Susan Coe; pages 34-5 to Penguin Education Illustration Department; page 38 to The British Museum; pages 43, 94, 99 to Camera Press Ltd; pages 44-5, 63 to Geoffrey Drury; page 46 to Philadelphia Museum of Art; page 59 to the John Hillelson Agency; pages 64, 78-9, 100-101 to Hans-Peter Klemenz; pages 66-7 to Keystone Press Ltd; pages 68-9 to MGM-EMI Distributors Ltd; page 74 to London News Service; pages 80-81 to the Tate Gallery; page 88 to Universitetets Oldsaksamling; page 93 to Hans Reich Verlag.

Every effort has been made to trace owners of copyright material, but in some cases this has not proved possible. The publishers would be glad to hear from any further copyright owners of material reproduced in *Other Worlds*.

List of Illustrations

Index of Authors, Translators and Collectors